D1322533

Managing people effectively

● ● ● ● ● ■ ●

JEAN CIVIL

CRAVEN COLLEGE
Skipton

WARD LOCK

To Eileen Geisler

A WARD LOCK BOOK

First published in the UK 1997
by Ward Lock
Wellington House
125 Strand
London
WC2 0BB

A Cassell Imprint

Copyright © Text Jean Civil 1997
Illustrations by Marilyn Paul and Richard Duszczak

All rights reserved. No part of this publication may be reproduced in any material
form (including photocopying or storing it in any medium by electronic means and
whether or not transiently or incidently to some other use of this publication) without the written permission of the copyright owner, except in accordance with the
provisions of the Copyright, Designs and patents Act 1988 or under terms of a
licence issued by the copyright Licensing Agency, 90 Tottenham Court Road,
London W1P 9HE. Applications for the copyright owner's permission to reproduce
any part of this publication should be addressed to the publisher.

Distributed in the United States
by Sterling Publishing Co., Inc.
38 Park Avenue South, New York, NY 10016-8810

A British Library Cataloguing in Publication Data block for this book may be
obtained from the British Library

ISBN 0 7063 7702 8

Designed, edited and produced by Pardoe Blacker Publishing Ltd,
Lingfield, Surrey RH7 6BL

Printed in Hong Kong by Midas Printing Limited

CONTENTS

■ Chapter 5: Is it because they can't — or is it

because they won't?

Acknowledgements

I would like to thank all the hundreds of managers I have met over the years as a Management Trainer, for their quotes, insights and stories. Hearing your stories made it possible for me to know and write about managers.

A special thank you to Jeannie Turnock for her computer skills in typing this book, and particularly for her excited interest and constant encouragement while I was writing it.

I am indebted to Norman Dickie, my co-trainer, for the witty – even rude – comments he made when he read the first drafts. He really helped me to focus.

I would also like to thank some great trainers with whom I have worked, Derek Marsh, Brenda Mallon, Colin Turner, Pablo Foster, Diane Brace and the late Bill Pasquerella, for their expertise, insights and humour on our training ventures.

Thanks go particularly to Mike Bryan, Ray Masters and the staff at Network Training. Then there are all the managers who have managed ME! In particular two terrific ones: Alan Chitty and Liz Balinger.

I am so grateful to my agent Alan Gordon Walker, who gave me confidence and made it all happen, and the superb staff at Pardoe Blacker.

Finally, but really by no means least, to my son Carl who did some word processing and commented on the contents, and my husband Geoff, who supported me emotionally and physically throughout the months of continuous work involved.

INTRODUCTION

Care, conflict, contention

People are your most expensive resource. Get your people skills right and the rest of your job becomes easier. You and your staff will be more motivated, which will bring joy into your workplace as well as improve efficiency and cost effectiveness. We spend so much of our life at work: enjoying work means enjoying life. Being an effective manager means being a saint, as it is likely that you are expected to manage a variety of people in a fair, unbiased, just and consistent way.

You may find your staff range from very interesting to boring; intelligent to stupid; energized to fatigued; old to young; motivated to demotivated and from genuine to phoney. They are likely to come from different social, economic and educational backgrounds, have different personalities, values, strengths, goals, needs, abilities and aspirations – but you have to command all the necessary skills to manage them.

What is more, even if you are able to reach someone, they could behave differently at other times because of personal issues or concerns. Yet you are still expected to manage them, regardless of your own background and needs.

You are expected at all times to be fair and to manage without prejudice, although it is impossible to avoid times when you feel prejudiced, when you do pre-judge how a person will act or respond to your requests.

You are expected to be fair, but again it is likely that there are occasions when you are unfair, when you do give more time to the people you like, or perceivably give more exciting or fulfilling jobs to your favourites. Yes, favourites: are you shocked, or are you already defending yourself with thoughts of 'I don't have favourites'? Be honest, for if you are not honest with yourself, then you will be unable to grow and move forward with this book or any other similar work.

It is a difficult job to be a manager – it is even more difficult to be an effective manager. You may have been promoted into the position of managing others without any training or guidance and may simply have to rely on your common sense, which is invaluable. Have you ever heard people make the comment about someone with loads of qualifications, who is supposedly so intelligent, that unfortunately they 'lack common sense'? So if you have common sense then you are half way there.

I wonder how good a manager you think you are? Terrific? Good? All right on some days? Not bad with paper, but not too happy with the people part of the job? Fairly useless most of the time? In fact, how did you become a manager? Was it part of your career plan, or are you still amazed that you have landed such a position? It may be that when you were at school you were told you were lacking in some aspect of academic ability, but look at you now. If only that teacher could see you today.

Or do you think that you have got the job under false pretences, because of who you know or by default? Perhaps you still recall how you fooled them at the interview and wonder if one day you will be found out. Well, whatever the reasons were for your appointment, you are now a manager and as such you will need to work as effectively as possible, regardless of the stress of trying to manage your staff more effectively.

There is, of course, a great deal written and documented

about stress at work. Is your job stressful? Perhaps you believe there is no such thing as stress, it is just life and some people cannot cope. Certainly, managing people is more stressful than managing paper. Maybe you have to manage some staff who appear stressed to you, who seem to have many personal problems that get in the way of their working effectively or efficiently. How are you supposed to manage these people? – after all, you are not a doctor.

There are numerous management books on the practical aspects of management but few on how to deal with your emotions or how to manage yourself when managing others. This workbook deals with the real issues of managing people. It looks at how to deal with your emotions at work, it even mentions sexuality, something that is unlikely to be found in other management books. Yet you probably use up to 50 per cent of your mental energy on your and other people's emotions. So I take specific 'people' issues that may arise for you, ask you to try to recognize your own present behaviour and suggest ways in which you may try to improve and develop your present skills.

Together we will consider some of the varying ways in which you can manage people more effectively, recognizing that people are individuals and their behaviour can vary. As a manager, there will be times when you will need to care, manage conflict or deal with contentious situations. So we will explore why it is easier for you to manage some people than others.

You will be asked to try to identify the kind of relationships that you are presently experiencing and why some of your communications go wrong. This book aims to give you practical suggestions of how to really listen, how to free and empower your staff and how to avoid making assumptions about them.

The subject which can cause great concern is that of managing conflict. You will be able to recognize your preferred style of dealing with conflict by completing a questionnaire, which is then analysed, showing different kinds of conflict that are likely to arise for you as a manager. You will find exercises giving you guidelines on how to use language succinctly and address conflict in a way that is effective and resolves issues. This is followed by tips on how you can deal with criticism.

When you have members of your team who are not performing up to the standards you expect, it is imperative that you address these situations. You will need courage, but it will pay off. Hence you will have to consider the question: 'Is it because they can't, or is it because they won't?' Hopefully, you will be able to access the evidence you used to reach your decision. Also, you may recognize what organizational causes may exacerbate unproductive behaviour.

Furthermore, you are likely to recognize the difference between team members who are incompetent or incapable and those you may need to discipline. This section ends with a comprehensive flow-chart that guides you through any formal procedures you may need to undertake. Although the subject is addressed, it is hoped that if you manage people in the ways that are suggested earlier, the need to discipline staff will be unlikely.

By the end of the book you will be able to understand more about your own behaviour and that of your staff, be able to listen and respond more accurately, support them at crisis points, and be a better communicator and more assertive. Hopefully you will be more skilled at managing issues of conflict and criticism. In addition, you will be able to tackle the daunting area of effectively managing staff who perform marginally, that is below some expected standard. You may also become more knowledgeable about the legally required formal procedures.

CHAPTER

1

Why do I find it easy to manage some people, but not others?

egardless of how senior or junior a manager you are, you will still have to manage yourself in order to manage others. Let us begin by highlighting your relationships with people at work. Forget for a moment *what* you have to manage and concentrate on *who* you have to manage. You only have so much energy and time in a working week and it is likely that you are spending a disproportionate amount of time on certain members of staff and very little on others. Your mental energy level (that is, the amount of energy you use on thinking or worrying about things) is consequently lowered.

You are highly likely to have a mixture of staff, some of whom you like and some you don't. There may be a few you find it very difficult to relate to. Some, on the other hand, get on with the job, take up little of your time, and are easy to work with. It is these people to whom you delegate responsibility since they appear to be achieving their targets successfully.

Others, however, always seem to want to talk to you about minute inconsequential details, fall behind on deadlines, lack drive or sparkle and seem to take up too much of your precious time. It is likely that you will always have such a mixture, but with astute management skills you can help move some of the people from the latter group into the former one.

Regardless of these two categories, there is probably something more fundamental going on in you. Something which you may be reluctant to discuss with others. Thoughts, emotions and attitudes that you hold towards staff in both groups.

In this chapter we are going to explore what it is about you and others that can lead to your being less effective with some staff while having the skills and the ability to work effectively with others. The first stage is to try to identify how you feel about the people you work with, whether they are people you manage or who manage you. The next stage is to identify what it is about you that may be creating some of the difficulties you experience. It probably comes down to your basic needs. Maybe you need to be liked, be right, be quick, be strong, or be seen to be in charge and always trying harder. Whatever drives you will have an effect on how you manage.

Below you will find several questionnaires which will enable you to identify certain behaviour in yourself and others. It is possible to change some of these behaviour patterns so that you can do your work better, thereby helping your staff to work better.

Perhaps you have negative feelings towards some staff.

Perhaps you work with some staff, both senior and junior to yourself, who you think have been promoted beyond their ability. At the same time, there are likely to be other people with whom you feel positive, enjoy their company, think that they are a 'good laugh', even possibly feel sexually attracted towards them or intellectually stimulated by them.

In order to begin to identify why it is easier for you to manage some people and not others, please complete the following questionnaires. You may find it helpful to begin by reflecting on what feelings you have towards your staff before being given the reasons as to why this might be so.

QUESTIONNAIRE 1

● ●

Who works well?

List the names of ten people you work with who would fall into one of the two categories listed on page 14. Try to put ten in each column. If you cannot think of ten, it does not matter; simply write down as many as you can.

A: Works well, pleased with their work	B: Do not really think that they work well
_____	_____
_____	_____
_____	_____
_____	_____
_____	_____
_____	_____
_____	_____
_____	_____
_____	_____
_____	_____

QUESTIONNAIRE 2

● ●

Please answer the following questions as honestly as you can.
There are no right or wrong answers.

1   Who do you like at work?

_____

_____

_____

_____

(If you are resistant to the word 'like' change it to 'get
on with' or 'enjoy working with' or 'find it easy to work
with'.)

2   Who do you dislike at work?

_____

_____

_____

_____

(Again, if you are querying the word 'dislike',
change it into your own preferred language 'gets up
some part of your anatomy' or 'have little rapport with'.)

3   Who do you trust at work?

_____

_____

_____

_____

(A belief that they will not betray you to others or relay
confidential disclosures.)

4 **Who have you trusted but now find that this trust has been broken or betrayed?**

_____

_____

_____

_____

(Find that the person you trusted has now broken that trust. If you cannot think of someone at work, what about outside work?)

5 **Who do you think has been promoted beyond their ability?**

_____

_____

_____

_____

(Even though they may have the 'qualifications'.)

6 **Who intellectually stimulates you?**

_____

_____

_____

_____

(Someone you can pit your wits against, or with whom you can enjoy stimulating banter and feel as though your brain is being stretched.)

7 **Who has a good sense of humour?**

_____

_____

_____

(Think of someone who makes you laugh or has an infectious kind of humour. Maybe they are bubbly and have the ability to cheer everyone up.)

8   Do you find anyone sexually attractive?

_____

_____

_____

_____

(This can be someone of the opposite or the same
gender, depending on your sexual orientation.)

9   Who do you have positive feelings towards?

_____

_____

_____

_____

(Those thoughts or comments like, 'I feel I've known you
for years ...'; 'We just seemed to get on so well right
from our first introduction or meeting ...')

10   Who do you have negative feelings towards?

_____

_____

_____

_____

(Those phrases like, 'There's something about him ...'; 'I
don't know what it is about her, but ...'; 'I can't put
my finger on it, but we just don't jell ...')

■ EXPLANATION

Now look at your list in Questionnaire 1 and see if the same names also appear in Questionnaire 2. If they do, then put a mark against the name. Any surprises? Check to see which list they appeared in: A or B in Questionnaire 1?

Now analyse the following ten questions from questionnaire 2

1 Did the people you like show up in column A? Yes ☐ No ☐

2 Did the people you dislike show up in column B? Yes ☐ No ☐

3 Did the people you trust show up in column A? Yes ☐ No ☐

4 Did the people you distrust show up in column B? Yes ☐ No ☐

5 Did the people you thought were promoted beyond their ability show up in column B? Yes ☐ No ☐

6 Did the people you have negative feelings towards show up in column B? Yes ☐ No ☐

7 Did the people you have positive feelings towards turn up in column A? Yes ☐ No ☐

8 Did the people you find sexually attractive show up in column A? Yes ☐ No ☐

9   Did the people you find
    intellectually stimulating show
    up in column A?   Yes ☐   No ☐

10. Did you find the people with a good   Yes ☐   No ☐
    sense of humour showed up in
    column A?

Have you found that most of the people you feel positive about appear in column A and those you feel negative towards in column B? Does this tell you anything? Read on for the analysis.

■ ANALYSIS

Having answered the questionnaire, consider the following reasons for your responses. Some may make sense to you, while others may be initially unacceptable. Try not to dismiss any ideas too quickly, but reflect on them. When you gain insight, sometimes it can be painful, but then learning can be painful. Is there any learning in the exercises you have just completed? Let us look at your answers:

1. Who do you like?

People we like usually share our values and belief systems. The name of the person you like probably shares yours, making it highly likely that you will find this person easier to manage, since you talk the same language or at least share some common values. This makes your starting point that much further along the line when explaining your requirements of them, issuing them with instructions or discussing new projects and ideas. You are starting from the same point and do not need to battle with trivia. You just know that they understand how, why, or on what basic beliefs your decisions have been made. This does not mean that you never disagree, but at least there is an understanding of each other's viewpoint.

2. Who do you dislike?

In contradistinction, the people you do not like probably do not share your value systems. For example, if they make racist, or sexist remarks, and you hold the concept of people's equality as a strong value, then it is more likely that you will find them difficult to manage. There are many other reasons for not liking them. You may simply not like their physical appearance or they may remind you of someone similar who you didn't like, and so on. You may see traits in them that you see in yourself. That is, traits that you don't like about yourself. Sometimes you may not like them because you believe that they are not very genuine.

You may feel insecure about your own ability and dislike someone who is more capable or more academically able than yourself. Perhaps they applied for the post you now hold and you still feel uncomfortable that you were chosen in preference to them. You may find problems with people who annoy you, patronize you, try to control you or imply that really they could do the job better.

3. Who do you trust?

The person you trust has probably shown you their vulnerable side and it is highly likely that you have reciprocated. They probably trust you. However good you are as a manager, there will be times when you will need support. Life may at times become difficult for you at home with family, friends or in your working relationships. So it is very positive that you have someone with whom you can share confidences in the knowledge that any information given to them will not be disclosed to others. Trust is usually two-way. You cannot expect people to trust you if you don't trust them. Equally, you won't trust them if they don't trust you, so you need to start by trusting your staff.

4. Has anyone broken or betrayed your trust?

Now you have identified someone who has broken your trust, think back to how this happened and how you have managed that relationship since. It is important that you deal with that broken trust, that you tell the person how you feel. Once trust has been broken, no matter how hard you both try to re-establish the same trusting relationship, it never reaches the same level. There is always an element of mistrust lingering in the background.

Think of someone at work or at home who has broken your trust in them. Did you try to work really hard at salvaging the relationship, tried to trust them again, but were unable to get back to the security and level of trust that you shared previously? Has that been your experience?

5. Who do you think has been promoted beyond their ability?

On what did you base your opinion of someone promoted beyond their ability? Perhaps they secured the position for which you applied. Maybe it is envy. Have they got the ear of someone YOU would like to impress, or do you think they were appointed under suspicious circumstances? Perhaps they were the friend or lover of the person who promoted them. Maybe there was a possible collapse of their previous appointment, so a new appointment was bestowed upon them to avoid their redundancy.

6. Does anyone stimulate you intellectually?

People need to be stimulated in order to work to their full poten-
tial. You need a challenge; both the right- and left-hand sides of
the brain need to be used. The right side of the brain is your
artistic side, the left side is the factual side. You need to give
yourself permission to use both, otherwise you may be right- or
left-hand side deprived. Spend more time with people who stim-
ulate you intellectually. It is like a tonic and can enable you to
grow and move in new ways. Recognize your need for intellec-
tual stimulus.

7. Who has a good sense of humour?

Humour can vary with culture, gender, age or specific situations. There can be a lot of game-playing in management:
pomposity, arrogance and power games. One of the most useful
assets you can have is a spontaneous sense of humour. There
will be times when you will need to relax, step back from the
pressures and try to see the funny side. Laughter is considered
by many doctors to reduce blood pressure and so help stave off
many serious diseases. So enjoy your work. Laugh, be spontaneous and have some fun in your job.

8. Is there anyone you find sexually attractive?

Management books do not discuss sexual relationships at work
but much energy is used on these feelings. While it is fine to feel
sexually attracted to people, it is how you behave that is important. Admitting to yourself how you feel is the first step and
working extra hard at being fair with all your staff is the second.

9. Who do you have positive feelings towards?

When you have positive feelings towards a certain individual,
you are likely to feel comfortable in their company. You may
be projecting on to that person the positive feelings you have

had towards someone else in your life (see the next question). It is often easier to manage the people you feel comfortable with than those with whom you do not feel so comfortable.

10. Who do you have negative feelings towards?

I have left this question until last because it will probably cause you more problems than the others. Feeling negative towards someone is not the best basis for a positive working relationship.

If you are having difficulty relating to someone and are experiencing negative feelings but cannot clearly see or understand why this is the case, then consider the fact that they remind you of someone else and that you are projecting this memory on to the other person. This means you relate to the 'shadow' rather than to the real person.

The memory could be activated by many different factors. Sometimes it could be someone's physical appearance, speech, religion, race, role, gender or attitude, that results in your negative feelings. Let us now look at each of these issues.

The importance of appearance

People's appearance creates all kinds of stereotyping and prejudice. How people dress may affect your feelings towards them. If you are a manager in a setting where a uniform is part of the culture, then some of this tension is removed, but even so, for some managers even a hairstyle can be a source of unease. Supposedly, wearing a jacket influences how people feel towards you: 80 per cent of what you say is believed. Other thoughts to consider are, if you want to look empowered as a woman, then tie your hair back, wear make-up and darker clothes, preferably suits and avoid peep-toed shoes and long earrings, as they are considered to lessen credibility. If you want to appear empowered as a man, wear a dark suit, lighter shirt and socks that match. For both genders, carry a smaller document case rather than a bulging briefcase. Supposedly, you are so organized that you or your secretary has just put into the bag the relevant papers for your day's work.

Physical appearance

People's physical appearance can be deceptive at the best of times. Have you ever wanted to ask for directions and looked around for a suitable person to ask? Then been surprised that the besuited, intelligent-looking person was aggressive and lacked clarity, whereas the youth with the scary orange tomahawk hairstyle, dressed in studded leathers, was gentle, concise and helpful? Then there are moustaches and beards. You may be stereotyping people because their facial hair makes them look like the villains you saw in childhood books, films and television programmes.

Speech

Speech and the language people use can also affect how you react to that person. Many managers would object to swearing or defamatory comments about work or home situations, but it is usually more subtle than that.

Speech might include using certain words that create a feeling of unease in you, or you may be using such words that affect how your staff relate to you. For instance, using words like working 'for' people, instead of working 'with' them; battle language like 'axe' the expenditure instead of 'reduce'; 'confront' or 'tackle' people instead of 'address'; 'problems' instead of 'issues' or 'concerns'; 'why' instead of 'what' or 'how'; 'ought' instead of 'could'; 'should' instead of 'may'; 'coloured' instead of 'black'. What words affect you and create negative feelings in you?

Some words are bound to be emotive, like 'cancer', but it may be difficult to find a replacement for them. At least think about them. The word 'redundancy' can create fear, unless someone is looking forward to retirement, or wanting to change jobs anyway. I find 'downsizing' an irritating word and not a positive replacement for 'redundancies' or 'reductions'.

As well as the words themselves, consider the way in which you speak. Many managers still have misconceptions about the difference between aggressive and assertive language. So you may be using the right words, but speaking in an abrupt, clipped way. Certain accents and dialects may irritate you. Your's may irritate your staff. You cannot do much about that, but at least be aware that you may be dismissing someone just because of the way they speak.

Body language
As well as your spoken language, there is also the factor of your body language. This is dealt with in detail in the next chapter.

Religion
The element of religion is deeply ingrained in many people. So much has been written and discussed about religion, yet it still remains the most explosive of subjects and very divisive in the way it can separate both families and nations. It is hardly surprising therefore, that you or others may have negative feelings towards someone whose religion is different, if your formative years were spent being indoctrinated as to your religious supremacy. Someone's religion may even affect your selection procedures for job interviews. It is essential that you become aware of the reasons behind your negativity towards certain people if you really want to manage effectively.

Races

People from different cultures and different races may create unease in you, again because of early childhood messages you received. Regardless of someone's culture, you will still find within any group of people some to whom you relate well and others with whom you find it difficult to jell. Within any race, including your own, it may well be that some people do not share your value systems. Prejudice is built on fear of the unknown and/or a lack of knowledge, and it is only when you bother to gain knowledge of a person that you can make a reasoned decision about them.

Certainly, in Great Britain, there are significantly more white than black managers.

Roles

People's roles can also create negative feelings in you. One reason may be that you think they do not deserve such a position. Or you may believe their personality is such that they are unfit to have a responsible role with the attitudes they hold. For example, someone who pays lip-service to equal opportunities, but also treats people with disdain and makes prejudiced comments when in your company.

Gender

It is well documented that more men than women hold managerial positions. Some men and some women will be happy with the imbalance of males to females, but others may feel aggrieved by the situation.

Where do you stand on this issue? As a woman you may think that you have been overlooked for promotion and that the job has been given to an inadequate man just because the culture is male-dominated and men make the decisions.

Equally, as a man you may think that you have been

overlooked for promotion and the job has been given to an inadequate woman just because the current trends are to look for woman managers in order to show how progressive the organization is. Both situations can lead to staff feeling cheated or betrayed.

The gender balance of your team may create negative feelings in you. If you feel more comfortable with a particular gender, you are likely to manage them more effectively. Your sexual orientation, however, need not necessarily dictate who you feel more comfortable with at work. There are many heterosexual men and women who prefer to work with men, while others prefer to work with women. Similarly, homosexual women or men may prefer to work with people of either the same or opposite sex. Try not to judge the whole male or female population on the basis of your experience of a handful of each sex who may have let you down. It is more likely that there are some women or men whom you feel negative towards, not because of their gender, but because of the numerous other reasons that have been discussed.

Attitude

Your attitudes can add to your mismanagement of staff. If people do not share your attitudes you need to be able to discuss this. Are you able to change your attitudes or are you intolerant of those staff who don't change theirs to yours? How can you change people's attitudes? To do this, you need to join them where they are and then try to bring them over to your viewpoint.

You may recall the difficulty initially experienced by the British government in getting people to use seat belts, when it was made illegal to drive without their use. They needed to change people's attitudes. At first they ran a television commercial with a peach which was being smashed by a hammer, symbolizing someone being smashed to pieces in a car accident. That was too far from people's attitude of mind to bring about any change in their behaviour and to persuade them to put on their seat-belts. So they had a well-known celebrity appear on television repeating a catchy phrase, 'Clunk, Click, Every Trip', and the public responded. It was closer to their own attitudes, and behaviour changed.

Some theorists reckon that you have to change attitudes before behaviour can change, while others argue that if you change people's behaviour then you change their attitudes. Debatable, but what do you believe? Do you try to change people's behaviour or attitudes? Or, preferably, both.

Your own attitude to your staff is crucial. If you are positive towards them they are likely to respond positively towards you, and the reverse is true. What is your attitude regarding loyalty to your staff? Do you have team loyalty? Or do you talk about them behind their backs, hoping to influence people's attitudes towards them or you? Loyalty has to be earned by both parties. So maybe you should start by talking *to* people, not *about* them.

Having looked at what might affect you consciously, that is physical appearance, speech, religion, race, role gender or attitude, let us consider what might affect you unconsciously.

You may be working with someone and experiencing an uncomfortable feeling but you are not sure why you feel this way, since they have not directly upset you. There could be many occasions when this feeling gets in the way of your working together effectively.

You may be asked to join a sub-committee on which this person sits, but feel reluctant. Or you may have to work on a project together, but make excuses that someone else would be a better choice. At lunch breaks, you may find yourself avoiding socializing with a particular group because this person is already part of that gathering.

It is important for you to be able to recognize the person casting this 'shadow', but how can you deal with the situation? When you experience uncomfortable feelings towards someone, try the next two exercises.

EXERCISE 1:
Shadowing

• •

The following exercise is to enable you to identify who you might be relating to unconsciously when you have very strong negative or positive feelings. Think of someone you feel negative about, and ask yourself the following questions:

Who do they remind me of?
(John? Mary? Mother? Headteacher? My first boss? etc.)
Write in the name that comes   _____
to mind. If they do not remind   _____
you of anyone go straight   _____
to Exercise 2   _____

In what ways is this person like (John etc.)**?**
Write in the way they are   _____
similar and the feelings that   _____
occur to you. For example: _____
Same age? Beard? Looks at   _____
me in the same way?   _____
Feel sexually threatened?   _____
Sexually excited? Makes me   _____
feel scared, put down or   _____
inferior? Has power over me?   _____

In what ways is the person <u>not</u> like (John, Mary, etc)**?**
Taller? More intelligent? Sense   _____
of humour? Different job? We   _____
only meet at work, etc. Put in   _____
all the details however trivial   _____
they may seem.   _____

EXERCISE 2

• •

This exercise enables you to discover who it is that is unconsciously affecting you and creating the negative or positive feelings you have towards them.

How does this person make me feel?

(Angry? Hurt? Excited? One
feeling is sufficient.) Write in
the feeling.

_____

_____

_____

_____

_____

_____

_____

Who else in my life has made me feel like this?

(Angry etc., – use the same word
you have used when asking the
previous question.)
Write in the name of a person
who has made you feel the
same way. Now you know who
they remind you of, complete
the rest of the exercise.

_____

_____

_____

_____

_____

_____

_____

Who do they remind me of?

(John? Mary? Mother?
Headteacher? My first boss? etc.)
Write in the name that comes
to mind. If they do not remind
you of anyone go straight to
the next question.

_____

_____

_____

_____

_____

In what ways is this person like (John etc.)?

Write in the way they are
similar and the feelings that
occur to you. For example,
Same age? Beard? Looks at me
in the same way? Feel sexually
threatened? Sexually excited?
Makes me feel scared, put down
or inferior? Has power over me?

_____
_____
_____
_____
_____
_____
_____

In what ways is the person not like (John, Mary, etc)?

Taller? More intelligent? Sense
of humour? Different job? We
only meet at work, etc. Put in
all the details however trivial
they may seem.

_____
_____
_____
_____
_____
_____
_____

■ EXPLANATION

By going through either or both of these exercises you make the 'shadow' change into a mosaic pattern, which then fragments and falls away from the person. This enables you to relate to the 'shadowless' person more effectively.

You will find this invaluable for clearing your thinking and being able to recognize that often it is you who has difficulty in relating, rather than your colleague, who is most probably unaware of how you feel towards him or her. If you feel uncomfortable with someone, for whatever reason, they are likely to feel the same towards you.

So now you can probably identify why you feel negative towards people: your line manager, other managers, or staff for whom you have some line managerial responsibility.

When you do identify people's 'shadows', it helps to say something to the individual such as 'You know, you remind me of my father, so sometimes you may find me responding to *him* rather than *you*'. This can be said in jest, but actually it is helping you to rid yourself of the unnecessary baggage which you are carrying around. Having looked at what might be happening to you in your different working relationships, the next chapter offers you the chance to identify what might be going wrong and how to rectify the situation.

CHAPTER

2

Why do some conversations go wrong?

Identifying the relationships

How many times have you said something, meaning well, but it has been interpreted as critical or someone has thought that you implied a totally different meaning or instruction? Usually what follows are recriminations. Each person thinks they are right and that the other did not listen or understand what was said.

▎Why do some conversations and communications go wrong?

'I didn't say that!' but the other person is sure that you did say that. It is not what we think we have said but what someone has heard.

The reason that some communications go wrong is perhaps because you forget to CHECK IT OUT.

■ Checking out skills

People often hear what they want to hear, so an important skill for you as a manager is to ask the other person what they think they have heard. If you find this difficult, you could try prefixing your request with something like:

'I just want to check we have both been talking about the same thing because sometimes I think I have said something but have not made my point clearly.'

Otherwise ask for clarification in a more direct way: for example, 'What do you think we have agreed?', or 'Having delegated this work to you, what do you think you now have to do in order to achieve our agreed deadlines?'

■ 'But I told you!'

Then there is the situation where a staff member comes to you as a manager to ask your permission or help with a certain issue or task, saying, for instance, 'How would you like me to start implementing the reorganization of the new staffing structure?' You reply 'But I told you'.

Equally, you may ask something of a member of your staff and they reply; 'But I told you'; however you didn't hear them. How much of the fault lies with you for not listening?

Listening skills

It is easy to listen when you are hearing what you want to hear; when you are not preoccupied with other thoughts; when you have time; maybe when you like the person; when you are free from interruptions. However, this is a luxury that many managers would love to experience. In order to listen effectively, and therefore to manage people effectively, it is essential that you acquire the skill of *active listening*. This means listening with your ears, eyes and heart.

Listening is a difficult, sophisticated skill, acquired with years of practice, starting with conscious awareness and moving into unconscious competence.

To describe these stages of conscious awareness and unconscious competence, here are four steps of learning new skills:

Diagram 1

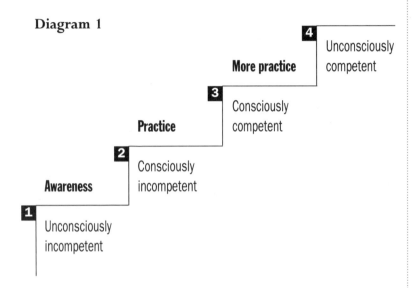

Step 1: Initially you are unaware of the importance of listening. You are *unconsciously incompetent*.

Step 2: With awareness comes the feeling of *incompetence*, the fear of not having heard everything, or concern at not understanding what is being said. Alongside this stage there may be feelings of incompetence about being unable to deal with the issue being raised.

Step 3: At this stage you are *consciously competent* at listening effectively but you are also consciously aware of all the skills needed for active listening; that is accepting body language, rapport, empathizing and reflecting. This stage can be difficult because there are so many things to think about, but it becomes easier with more practice at active listening.

Step 4: Now you are able to listen actively without thinking about all the skills required. It has become second nature, like so many other skills you have mastered. You are now *unconsciously competent*.

Let's demonstrate these steps in another way. If you have learned to drive at some point in your life, think back to when you first learned to drive. If you are not a driver then think about another skill you have already acquired, for example learning how to swim. The first stage was being *unconsciously incompetent*. You had no specific idea how cars were driven; they just moved about with someone driving them. As you were taught new skills, you reached an awareness of what was really required of you: the stage of being *consciously incompetent*. Can you recall all those skills you were expected to have but remember instead feeling disjointed, lacking understanding and feeling and knowing you were *incompetent*. You did not seem to have enough arms or legs to do all the things that were expected of you.

With practice you then became *consciously competent*, provided that you were thinking about what you were doing, aware that you needed to concentrate. Now you can perform the skill – driving or swimming – from your state of *unconscious competence;* you do not have to think about how to drive, you just do it.

Let us see how effective you are at listening. How do you know if you are a good listener and what effective listening skills are? At this stage answer Questionnaires 3 and 4 and then consider the analysis of how you can improve your listening skills.

QUESTIONNAIRE 3
How good a listener are you?

• •

The following questions are to help you to become self aware. Be honest in order to gain the most from the exercise. Please do not say to yourself 'It depends', as this will only block you. So either think of a particular management conversation you have had with a member of staff or think generally about your most likely responses.

		YES	NO
1	Are you able to change your degree of listening from social interaction to active listening?	☐	☐
2	Do you sit and think how long-winded some of your staff are?	☐	☐
3	Do you want to interrupt with questions for yourself rather than for the staff member?	☐	☐
4	Would that help?	☐	☐
5	Are you patient when listening?	☐	☐
6	Are you aware of other people's feelings?	☐	☐
7	Are you aware of your own feelings?	☐	☐
8	Do you understand what is being said?	☐	☐
9	Are you aware of what is not being said?	☐	☐
10	Do you check out and reflect what you are hearing with the staff member?	☐	☐

How did you do?: Effective active listening

1 Supporting

It is important to recognize that the degree of listening required for social interaction is far lower than that which is needed when you are trying to help someone. In order to raise your expertise at listening you need to be person-centred. For instance, try to avoid joining in with your own thoughts or experiences. For example, avoid phrases like: 'You think you have problems, you ought to hear mine.' Give people the opportunity to say what they want to say, not what you want to hear. Social interaction is two-way talking, whereas when you are helping someone to resolve their concerns it is mainly one-way talking, that is, from them, not you. So you need to be able to SUPPORT, e.g., 'Yes, that sounds very positive'.

2 Clarifying

It can be really difficult listening to someone who is longwinded, especially if you are the 'hurry up' type of manager. You may find yourself thinking, 'I wish you would get to the point'. So you need to be able to CLARIFY, e.g., 'So what is the point you are making?'

3 Constructing

When you are listening to someone there may be many questions you want to ask. You need to ask yourself, 'Is this question for me, or is it for the person I am listening to?' So many questions are for the benefit of the manager rather than for that of the staff member and are designed to please rather than to add value. If the desired outcome is to get them to talk, then ask questions for the other person if you want them to develop their thoughts.

So as well as constructing questions that are for the person to whom you are listening, you also need to get them to *construct* how things will happen, for example, 'Do you have plans as to how you might achieve that?' or 'What would you like to happen?'

4 Disagreeing

If you ask questions for yourself you are likely to block or 'bind' the other person. They have to think about your needs or the expected answers. So try not to interrupt because you disagree or by asking questions for yourself. Give them the opportunity to air their thoughts. This 'frees' your staff. However, this does not mean that you then accept everything that is said. You are certainly demonstrating that you have been listening, even when you *disagree*, e.g., 'I understand your reasoning', 'I am not convinced' or, 'I cannot agree with that!'

5 Confirming

It is important to be patient when you are listening. You may be giving out signs that you are bored, hurried or irritated. If your staff pick up these signs, they are likely to feel blocked, you bind them rather than free them. So give them time and then *confirm* what has transpired, e.g., 'So we agree that . . .'

6 Empathizing/Non-verbalizing

It is essential to be aware of the other person's feelings if you are to be able to demonstrate active listening. It is often the skill that needs the most practice and attention. Being aware is one thing, but feeling empathy can be more difficult. There is a big difference between empathizing and sympathizing with someone. The language used around the words are good indicators of the difference. We *empathize with* but *feel sympathy towards*. Being sympathetic is to think 'that must be difficult', whereas to empathize is to actually feel the person's anguish or enjoyment. To empathize you need to be able to 'walk in someone else's shoes', listen through their ears, see through their eyes, understand from their frame of reference. In other words, feel their feelings.

So, it is important to *empathize*, not only with feelings but also in demonstrating your empathy non-verbally. You will appear to empathize if you have an open body posture and attentive, accepting eye contact, create a rapport, keep your body still and give an occasional nod. You do not need a heart transplant to know how it works, but it might help. Even though you may not have had the experience that someone is telling you about, you are very likely to have experienced their feelings. So you can empathize with their situation. In order to empathize you need to listen with your ears, with your eyes, and above all, with your heart.

7   Criticizing

While it is necessary for you to be aware of other people's feelings, it is also imperative to recognize your own feelings, which may sometimes get in the way of your listening. If you are angry or hurt by what is being said, then it is unlikely that you will hear someone else. So you will need to be able to express how you feel. Remember, people cannot argue with how you feel. They can, however, argue with how you think. So, sometimes you will need to be able to *criticize*, e.g., 'I feel concerned/angry when you treat customers that way.'

8   Interpreting

When people talk to you, or even at you, you may not understand them. If you are concerned about appearing stupid, you may just smile and nod. It would be far more beneficial if you said, 'I don't understand'. The speaker would certainly feel listened to in that you are saying that you want to understand. It is highly unlikely that you will understand everything your staff or anyone else says to you. You could try using responses that *interpret* what is being said to you, e.g., 'So are you suggesting that?'

9   Testing

Many managers claim to have the skill to listen to what is being said, but few are able to hear what is *not* being said. That is often regarded as your being 'perceptive' or 'intuitive'. There are many clues to what people are not saying to you. A big give-away can be their body language. So it is possible for you to add to your perception or intuition by *testing* and revealing what is not being said but what you are hearing. 'Would it be right to say that ...?' or, 'If we did this then are you saying that...?' or, 'What you are not saying but what I am picking up is...'

10 Reflecting

Sometimes you may listen attentively but you may have misheard or misunderstood for many reasons. Therefore *reflect* and *check out* periodically to ensure that what you have heard is what has been said, e.g., 'Let me see if I've understood you...' or, 'So what I am hearing is...'

To summarize, there are so many tips on how to listen, but if you try to listen to the 'music behind the words' you will probably become a superb listener.

How did you do?

Now check the following synopsis. Cover the answers and see if you can remember the ten suggestions.

1	SUPPORTING	Yes, good idea; sounds very positive.
2	CLARIFYING	Please explain the point you are making? So, you are saying. . . .
3	CONSTRUCTING	Do you have plans as to how you might achieve that? What would you like to happen?
4	DISAGREEING	I am not convinced. I cannot agree with that.
5	CONFIRMING	So, we agree that ...
6	EMPATHIZING	Non-verbal rapport, occasional nod, feeling their feelings.
7	CRITICIZING	I feel concerned when you treat customers that way.
8	INTERPRETING	So, are you suggesting that ...?
9	TESTING	Would it be right to say that ... If we did this, then ...?
10	REFLECTING	Let me see if I've understood you ... So, what I'm hearing is ...

QUESTIONNAIRE 4
What specifically do you do?

• •

1   When listening do you help your staff to express them-
    selves or hinder them. Do you free them or 'bind' them?

    _____

    _____

    _____

2   If you 'free' them, how precisely?

    _____

    _____

    _____

3   If you 'bind' them, how precisely?

    _____

    _____

    _____

4   What do you do when you are trying to help someone
    with a problem, rather than just chatting?

    _____

    _____

    _____

5   What could you say to someone to help them come to
    the point?

    _____

    _____

    _____

6   How do you try to 'read' the emotions of others?

_____

_____

_____

7   If you don't understand, what do you say or do to clarify
     the situation?

_____

_____

_____

8   How do you know the staff member is not listening?

_____

_____

_____

9   How does the staff member know when you are not
     listening?

_____

_____

_____

10   How do you check out that what is said is what you are
     both hearing?

_____

_____

_____

Having completed the questionnaires, what skills do you now think you have already which make you an effective, listening manager?

_____

_____

_____

_____

_____

_____

_____

_____

_____

_____

_____

Check your list against the ten behaviours which indicate effective active listening.

Some staff talk freely: others don't

Freeing your staff

In order to free your staff, you need to give them permission to speak freely to you about their job, relationships, concerns, need for support, aspirations and stresses, as well as to celebrate their successes, without the fear that you may be judging them as someone who is not coping very well, as conceited or as a 'moaner'. You will find this difficult, since most managers are judging or appraising staff with each meeting in which they are involved. Nevertheless, if you can free them to be honest with you then the rewards will be worthwhile.

Good active listeners do not need to say anything or move their heads, as they are sending messages all the time that they are actively listening (if they really are listening and not day-dreaming). So keep still, have an open body position and think about the other person and not yourself.

Binding your staff

On the other hand you may be binding your staff. This is sending messages to them that if they put their heads above the parapet they may get them shot off. You may be known for the way in which you bear grudges or talk about people behind their backs while being pleasant to their faces. Your staff may be anxious about how you respond to new ideas, complaints or even successes. Hence they may feel that you block or bind their honest viewpoints.

A poor listener will behave in some of the following ways:

Interrogating	Interrupting	Distracted
Ordering	Directing	Commanding
Warning	Admonishing	Threatening
Moralizing	Preaching	Imploring
Judging	Criticizing	Sarcasm
Ridiculing	Humiliating	Blaming

Active listening

If you are listening actively, this involves empathy and acceptance of the speaker and means that you are working from the attitude that you are both people with different feelings and maybe different perceptions. You need to have a positive regard for both yourself and the other person. When you are actively listening you are saying with your body and responses:

- I can empathize with what you are feeling.

- I understand how you are seeing things now.

- I am interested and concerned about what you have to say.

- I am not judging you.

- You do not need to feel afraid of my censuring what you are disclosing.

How do your staff see you?

Listening is a difficult, sophisticated skill acquired through conscious development and turned with practice into a smooth response. To be a good listener is not a natural state. Unfortunately some of your staff to whom you talk may not want to listen to you because:

1   They think they have something better to say.

2   They already have the answer to what they know to be the problem.

3   They have no reason or motive to listen to you.

4   They do not like you or what you represent.

5   They want to trap you.

6   They do not like what you are saying to them.

7   They are distracted or they have no immediate problems.

8   They understand more quickly than you can speak.

9   They are filtering your message for their own agendas.

10 They are thinking about what they are going to say next.

When your staff are actively listening to you, it may be because:

1   They are consciously trying to listen.

2   They like or admire you.

3   They think that they have something to say but are waiting for you to finish.

4   They think that a response is expected.

5   They believe that you might say something from which they can learn.

6   They are not experiencing any other distractions.

7   They are wondering if there are promotions or redundancies involved.

8   They are interested in your comments.

9   They value your opinion.

10 They enjoy working with you.

3

How do I handle conflict?

ow do you handle and manage conflict? As a manager there will be times when you wonder whether to say anything about a certain issue, or whether simply to ignore it. This decision can be difficult for all kinds of reasons. Your personality, your status, your relationship with the person involved, your security of tenure or your state of health, can all play a part in the decision making process.

In the previous chapters you may have recognized how your personality could affect the way you tend to relate to other people. So by now you will be more self-aware as to how you are likely to manage conflict at work.

If you are status conscious, you may feel positive about dealing with conflict between yourself and your staff, but anxious about sorting out conflict between yourself and your line manager.

The the kind of relationship you have with the person concerned is important. Maybe you are friends and this makes it either more difficult or, perhaps, easier for you to handle a difficult situation. Either way, it influences your decision. Whether you like or dislike the person will have some bearing on whether you decide to say anything or ignore it.

Your decision may also be affected by the current working climate. If several staff cutbacks are being mooted, then you may feel anxious about the security of your own job and decide to keep quiet.

The most likely influence is probably your state of health. If you are feeling positive about yourself you will want to deal with the conflict, but if you are feeling under the weather or have had an argument with someone at work or at home, then you will probably withdraw from what you will see as more problems.

Conflicts of varying kinds will always be found when you are in a managerial position. There may be a conflict of goals or targets, either within yourself, or between you and your staff. Also, there could be conflict between different people and different sections within your business or organization. (Each of these is addressed in more detail in the next chapter.)

The next stage is to look at how you could try to manage conflict within five different settings: conflict within yourself; between two people for whom you have some responsibility; within a group or a team; within the organization, and lastly conflict between you and one other person.

Then we look at specific skills for addressing conflict. Particular emphasis is put on language skills and how to handle criticism. What to say and how to say it.

In order to identify your present style of managing conflict, first complete Questionnaire 5: Handling conflict, and then Questionnaire 6: The A–Z of managing conflict.

QUESTIONNAIRE 5
Handling conflict

● ●

	Yes	No
1 Do you dislike conflict?	☐	☐

2   List five words that describe 'conflict' to you:

_____

_____

_____

_____

_____

3   What feelings do you associate with conflict?

_____

_____

_____

4   With whom are you most likely to come into conflict?
(Identify by position or by name of an individual).

a)   At work   _____

_____

_____

b)   Outside work   _____

_____

_____

5   What are the three most likely situations that cause conflict for you?

1) _____

2) _____

3) _____

6   If you have no conflicts (or very few) what may you deduce about:

1) yourself

_____

2) the staff with whom you work

_____

3) your relationship with your line manager

_____

7   How do you tend to resolve conflict?

	Yes	No
By my people skills	☐	☐
By negotiating with the person	☐	☐
By saying what I want	☐	☐
By talking to others about the situation	☐	☐
By looking for another job	☐	☐
By compromizing	☐	☐
By grumbling to others	☐	☐
By avoiding issues	☐	☐
By attacking others	☐	☐
By being pleasant to other people	☐	☐

8   Complete the statement by ticking the appropriate box:

'In conflict situations when I am the leader, generally...'

	Yes	No
I lose	☐	☐
I win	☐	☐
Both win or neither wins	☐	☐

9   The reason for the former is because I

_____

_____

_____

10   When I manage conflict with another person,
     the skills I use are:

_____

_____

_____

QUESTIONNAIRE 6

The A–Z of managing conflict

● ●

Now complete this important questionnaire, but before doing so, let me explain how it is organized. First of all you will find 20 pairs of questions labelled A–T. Detailed instructions are given before the list appears. Then you have six multiple choice questions labelled U–Z. Detailed instructions are given just prior to the U–Z part of the questionnaire. These choices are made up of different scenarios which could occur at work. Complete all the questions from A–Z before looking at the scoring sheet.

When you complete the questionnaire decide on one setting, either at work or at home, but do not move between the two. If you want to do both home and work, then go through the questionnaire (A–T) twice, maybe using different coloured pens to distinguish your scores quickly, first thinking about work, then home situations. You may find that your behaviour differs and this in itself could be an interesting outcome for you to think about. If you do choose to do this, then remember not to look at the scoring analysis until you have completed both work and home settings. If you want to concentrate only on how you behave at work, then simply work through from A–Z.

You have twenty pairs of statements labelled A to T. Select, by circling one from each pair of statements. Think carefully which is the nearest to your own behaviour or attitude.

I realize that you may think that neither option is what you are likely to do, but answer as honestly as you can.

Do not select the one which you think is the 'right' answer. Work quickly, answer every pair in order and do not look back at your answers. Be honest, otherwise you only cheat yourself.

Circle either the ★ or ☆ from each pair of statements:
e.g. ★ I like to get my own way in a conflict situation.
      ☆ I like to find a solution so that the other person feels good.

If neither of these statements is precisely what you believe, then choose the one which is the closest to your own beliefs or values. Hence, circle the ★ if you prefer to get your own way, or circle the ☆ if you prefer to find a solution so that the other feels good.

The A–Z of managing conflict (A–T)

A ★ Attaining my goals is my priority.
☆ I believe it is important to be open about my concerns.

B ★ I let people know what I think and like them to do likewise.
☆ In conflicting situations I like to win.

C ★ I prefer to agree rather then to argue.
☆ I keep things to myself to avoid trouble.

D ★ I like to be liked so I tend to smooth over conflict.
☆ I keep away from hostile people.

E ★ I think that both parties should give up something.
☆ I believe I should stick to my views.

F ★ I believe my objectives are right.
☆ I try to find a middle ground.

G ★ I do not believe in initiating ways of resolving conflict.
☆ I try to resolve conflict by compromise.

H ★ I am moderately concerned about other people's conflict.
☆ I do not like looking directly at people when conflict arises.

I ★ I use strong direct language.
☆ I smile a lot even when I am anxious.

J ★ I accept other people's views rather than cause trouble.
☆ Once I know I'm right I defend my position.

K ★ I believe in giving in a little to find a solution.
☆ I like to go along with other people's ideas.

L ★ I like being nice and co-operative with people.
☆ I think both parties should give and take.

M ★ I let time take its course and conflict usually
disappears.
☆ When conflict arises I can be hostile.

N ★ I try to get people to do it my way.
☆ I try not to worry about people's differences
of opinion.

O ★ I get everything out into the open as soon as possible.
☆ I leave the scene and let them get on with it.

P ★ I avoid people who cause conflict.
☆ I think that resolving conflict makes for better
relationships.

Q ★ I prefer not to argue but to look for the best solution
for both parties.
☆ I do not mind giving up some of my goals if the
other person also forgoes some of their goals.

R ★ I say what I feel and invite the other person to do
likewise.
☆ I believe that neither of the parties can expect to get
it all their own way.

S ★ I would rather go along with what is asked of me
than challenge it.
☆ I believe solutions can be found to conflict so that
both parties win.

T ★ I am not satisfied until all the tensions and negativity
have been resolved.
☆ I think having good relationships with people is better
than getting my own way.

Now continue with U–Z. Read the following scenarios which involve different kinds of work conflict. Choose one of the following five responses that you think is your most *likely* type of behaviour or attitude, then circle the symbols ▼ ♦ ● ▲ or ■. Again, be honest, do not choose what you consider to be the 'right' or the best answer.

The A–Z of managing conflict (U–Z)

U You are asked to work overtime on a specific day, but you do not want to, as you have made other plans.
   Do you say:

   ▼ Yes, I will stay.

   ♦ I could stay for a short while, but I can't do it all.

   ● Yes, no problem, I'll cancel my other arrangements.

   ▲ No, I need more notice.

   ■ No, but I could stay tomorrow and complete the jobs, if that would help you. Can we agree time off now which would suit both of us?

V You are receiving complaints from several members of your team about the behaviour of one team member.
   Do you:

   ● Smile at the person concerned and ask how they are.

   ♦ Suggest that the rest of the team do a little extra work to cover.

■ Call the team together and ask them to voice their concerns about team dynamics or responsibilities.

▼ Say nothing.

▲ See the person concerned and tell them to perform to standard, otherwise they will face the sack.

W You have to make five redundancies with remuneration. Do you:

■ Talk to all staff about the redundancies. Ask for volunteers first, then draw up a possible list after consultation with the staff.

▼ Do nothing, hoping things might change.

♦ Suggest to your superior that you could make two redundancies and put five on half-time working.

▲ Decide which five you want to go, without taking action.

● Worry about each person, consider their personal home life and how they will suffer.

X Two staff are complaining to you about the conflict between them. Each comes to you separately and moans about the other. Do you:

▼ Take no notice.

▲ Say that you are not there to sort out relationships, that you have more important targets to achieve.

■ Bring the two of them together and ask them to tell each other what the issues are, and in what ways they can be resolved. Observing the process rather then intervening.

● Agree with each person that it must be difficult. Let them know that you are glad they feel they can talk to you.

◆ Suggest they do the easy jobs and forget the area of conflict.

Y You are experiencing personal, family or relationship problems. Do you:

■ Recognize that you are suffering from inner conflict. Explain to your line manager that there are difficulties and that it may be necessary for you to have some time away from work, which you will make up.

▼ Say nothing.

▲ Stay at work and involve yourself in frantic activity.

● Talk with someone you like to gain reassurance that it is not your fault.

◆ Tell half-truths; consider taking sick leave.

Z You are experiencing unjust treatment, bullying,
or harassment (decide which) from someone at work.
Do you:

● Try to be nice to them. Exchange pleasantries each
time you see the person.

◆ Think, 'Well, they can be all right some of the time,
so that should be enough'.

■ Talk to them about the behaviour you have *observed*,
tell them how you *feel* and say what you *need* in
terms of their treatment of you.

▼ Avoid the person.

▲ Tell their line manager and suggest that they
should leave.

Discover your present style of managing conflict

These are the instructions on how to transfer your answers to the scoring sheet:

Questions A–T

Enter your answers under the relevant columns 1 to 5. Do this by circling the black star or white star under the indicated place in columns 1, 2, 3, 4 or 5.

For example:

Look at your answer to question A. If you selected the ★ response, then circle the black star sign under Column 4. Alternatively, if you have selected the ☆ response, then circle the white star sign under Column 5. Do this for all the questions up to T.

Questions U–Z

Then go on to scoring questions U–Z. Put a circle around the marker selected under the appropriate column 1, 2, 3, 4 or 5.

For example:

If your response to question U is the sign ● (Yes, no problem, I'll cancel my other arrangements) then put a circle under column 2 around the marker ●.

Finally, add the number of circles in columns 1, 2, 3, 4 and 5 to find your five separate scores.

Then transfer these five circled total scores into the five circles on diagram 2 below; i.e., the score in column 1 should be written in circle number one AVOIDING (OSTRICH) and so on for all five circles. Now look at diagram 3 and read on.

Managing people effectively

Table 1

Questions	Column 1	Column 2	Column 3	Column 4	Column 5
A				★	☆
B				☆	★
C	☆	★			
D	☆	★			
E			☆	★	
F			☆	★	
G	★		☆		
H			★		
I		☆		★	
J		★			
K		☆	★		
L		★	☆		
M	★			☆	
N				★	
O	☆				★
P	★				☆
Q			☆		★
R			☆		★
S		★			☆
T		☆			★
U	▼	●	♦	▲	■
V	▼	●	♦	▲	■
W	▼	●	♦	▲	■
X	▼	●	♦	▲	■
Y	▼	●	♦	▲	■
Z	▼	●	♦	▲	■
TOTAL CIRCLED					

■ How to handle conflict – matrix graph

Diagram 2

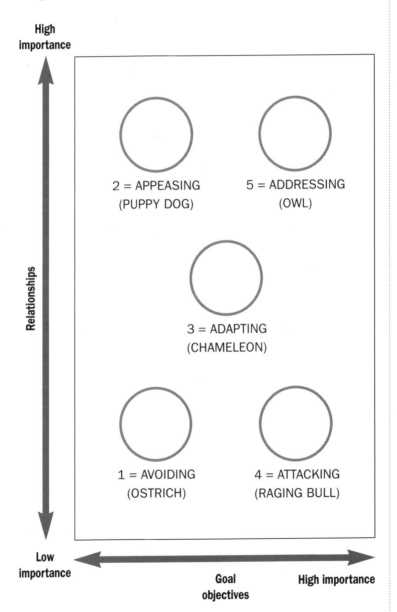

Diagram 3

High importance

Relationships

Puppy dog

Owl

Chameleon

Ostrich

Raging bull

Low importance

Goal objectives

High importance

1 THE OSTRICH (Avoiding)

Ostriches withdraw and hide their heads in order to avoid conflicts. They give up their personal goals and relationships. They stay away from the issues over which the conflict is taking place and from the people they are in conflict with. Ostriches believe it is hopeless to try to resolve conflicts. They feel helpless. They believe it is easier to withdraw (physically and psychologically) from a conflict than to face it.

2 THE PUPPY DOG (Appeasing)

To puppy dogs, the relationship is of great importance, while their own goals are of little importance. Puppies want to be accepted and liked by other people. They think that conflict should be avoided in favour of harmony and believe that conflicts cannot be discussed without damaging relationships. They are afraid that if the conflict continues, someone will get hurt and that would ruin the relationship. They give up their goals to preserve the relationship. Puppies say, 'I'll give up my goals and let you have what you want in order for you to like me.' Puppies try to smooth over the conflict for fear of harming the relationship

3. THE CHAMELEON (Adapting)

Chameleons adapt and change according to their surroundings. They are moderately concerned with their own goals and about their relationships with other people. Chameleons seek a compromise. They give up part of their goals and persuade the other person in a conflict to give up part of their goals. They seek a solution to conflicts where both sides gain something – the middle ground between two extreme points. They are willing to sacrifice part of their goals and relationships in order to find agreement for the common good. Many managers think that compromise is the best solution. This is not true, because compromise means that neither party feels satisfied. If you have a partner who wishes to sleep with the curtains open and you want to sleep with them closed, then a compromise would mean one side of the curtains is open and the other closed so that neither party feels happy.

4   THE RAGING BULL (Attacking)

Raging Bulls try to overpower opponents by forcing them to accept their solution to the conflict. Their goals are highly important to them and the relationship is of minor importance. They seek to achieve their goals at all costs. They are not concerned with the needs of other people. They do not care if other people like or accept them. Raging Bulls assume that conflicts are settled by one person winning and one person losing. They want to be the winner. Winning gives the bull a sense of pride and achievement. Losing gives them a sense of weakness, inadequacy and failure. They try to win by attacking, overpowering, overwhelming and intimidating other people.

5.   THE OWL (Addressing)

Owls highly value their own goals and relationships. They view conflicts as problems to be solved and seek a solution that achieves both their own goals and the goals of the other person in the conflict.

Owls see conflict as improving relationships by reducing tension between two people. They try to begin a discussion that identifies the conflict as a problem. By seeking solutions that satisfy both them

THE OWL (continued)

selves and the other person, and maintain the relationship. Owls are not satisfied until a solution is found that achieves their own goals and the other person's goals. They are not satisfied until the tensions and negative feelings have been fully resolved; they are assertive but not aggresive.

So if you want to manage conflict, try to model yourself on the wise owl!

CHAPTER **4**

How do I resolve conflict?

Having completed the questionnaire, you are probably clearer about the way in which you tend to handle conflict. So let us begin by identifying the different kinds of conflict and then consider positive working practices to enable you to resolve conflict more effectively.

There will be times, as a manager, when you will become aware of some kind of conflict that is taking place in the workplace and you will need to decide whether to say something, or to ignore it. Here are examples of five different kinds of conflict that you, as manager, or your staff, may experience.

Five types of conflict
Inner conflict
Conflict between two individuals
Conflict within a team
Conflict within the organization
Conflict with another person

Inner conflict

First, there is Inner Conflict. There are often two opposing inner thoughts which create inner conflict. 'What I am expected to do as a manager' versus 'What I really want to do'. You may be expected to dismiss someone for financial reasons but this may concern you deeply as you are aware of the devastating affect this will have on that person. The reason you are given for the dismissal is to save money and yet, simultaneously, you are aware of the excessive amounts of money being spent by the Directorate on expenses and first-class trips overseas.

So you experience 'cognitive dissonance' that is, two conflicting pieces of information that destroy your equilibrium. In order to reduce your own inner conflict and find inner harmony, you start to rationalize.

Think of a pair of Shylock-type scales. If you are a smoker you know about the physical affects on your health, so the scales are out of balance, weighed down on one side with negative information like: 'It's bad for my lungs', 'I smell like an ashtray', 'My colleagues resent my smoking' and so on. In order to create an equal balance of the two scales, you need to load the other side with positive information. 'Well, I don't take heroin', 'I smoke the brands with the lowest tar and nicotine content', 'It keeps me slim', 'I am a much more relaxed person than my stressed non-smoking colleague', 'I don't drink alcohol which is more harmful' and so on. By doing this the scales become balanced, which then creates some inner harmony for your decision to choose to smoke.

Similarly, at work, thinking about dismissing the member of staff feels negative, so you rationalize with the positive thoughts, 'Well, rather you than me', 'There are still jobs available for good workers', 'The money spent on expenses may bring in more business, hence more secure jobs'.

Eventually, you can go through the process of dismissal with less inner conflict.

Suspecting someone of stealing also creates inner conflict. Unless you have firm evidence you may continue to distrust someone but hope that you are wrong. You feel betrayed, especially when you have been helpful and supportive towards them.

It is likely that at some point in your career you will have inner conflict about allocating your time between work and home. Your partner makes demands on you, at the same time you have deadlines to meet at work. The phrase 'You think more of that job than you do of me' may be familiar to you.

Depending on your age, values and personal family circumstances, you may choose to forgo promotion for the quality of home life.

EXERCISE 3
Easing inner conflict
● ●

One way of trying to ease inner conflict is to write down your concerns and try to resolve some of the 'cognitive dissonance' (internal conflict). Below (Table 2) you will find three columns headed OPTIONS, OUTCOMES, FEELINGS.

In column one, *Options*, write down and number all the options you have; do not censor them at this stage. Just write down everything that comes to mind regardless of whether you think that you would like to do that or not.

Then move to column 2 headed *Outcomes*. Looking at each option, write down the outcome of each of the options, numbering them in relation to the numbers allocated for *Options*. Avoid including any feelings. Now cover up the first column of *Options* so that you do not refer to it. Do not cheat.

Then in column 3, *Feelings*, write down your feelings to the numbered *Outcomes*. (Do not turn to the *Options* to see what the *Outcomes* relate to.) Number your *Feelings* to correspond with the same numbers as the *Options*. Then underline the *positive* feelings.

Now uncover column 1, *Options* and see which *Options* give you the most *positive,* happiest feelings. This is the best option for you to take: if you choose to follow this, then you will have dealt with some of your cognitive dissonance. For example, 'Shall I apply for the new job?'

Here is an example so that you can see the range of possibilities. Then complete your own table, Table 3. Use whatever question is applicable for you.

Table 2

Options	Outcomes	Feelings
1. Yes, apply.	1. Great job, more responsibility, just what I want.	1. Really happy
	1 Might not get the job.	1. Upset
	1. People will know I'm looking for another job.	1. Concerned
	1. They may not promote me if they think I'm on the lookout for something else.	1. Fine

	1. Solve financial problems.	1. Great
2. No, don't apply.	2. I'll never know if I would have got it.	2. Restless
	2. Will have financial problems.	2. Awful
3. Just send for the forms.	3. Might give me some ideas.	3. Doesn't matter
	3. Waste of time.	3. Annoyed
4. Show job to boss and ask for comparable rise.	4. Boss may loose respect for me.	4. Worried
	4. Boss may give me a salary increase.	4. Good
5. Apply, do not tell partner.	5. If I get an interview what will I say to partner?	5. Worried
	5. There would be a row if partner found out.	
6. Don't apply. Tell partner that I have.	6. Partner might meet someone and ask about the job. Another row if found out I had lied.	6. Unhappy

Now use this table to resolve any inner conflict that you may be experiencing

Table 3

Options	Outcomes	Feelings

Inner conflict – 'Shall I apply for the new job?'
As you can see, the positive feelings underlined of 'Really happy', 'Fine', 'Great', all related to option 1 to apply for the job. The only other positive feeling of good referred to getting more money in option 4. You are likely to gain this anyway if you got the new job.

So the inner conflict is resolved – apply for the job. Of course if you don't get it, then you might have to start the whole exercise over again as to how to deal with your inner conflict of failing the interview. Never mind, still apply.

Conflict between two individuals
There may be conflict *between two individuals* for whom you have a managerial responsibility.

One member of staff (let's call him James) comes to you and grumbles about another member of your staff, say Susan. You may find yourself agreeing with James that Susan's behaviour is unacceptable. Then Susan comes to complain about James's bullying behaviour, and you find yourself agreeing with Susan about James's unacceptable behaviour. You start to collude with both parties. Bad news. This is poor management. It is important that you bring the two people together to resolve the issue.

Avoid taking sides with either against the other. Examples of the different kinds of behaviour in this situation are given in The A–Z of Managing Conflict Questionnaire, question Z (in Chapter 3).

Offer each of them the opportunity to say how they see the situation, how they feel, what they think and what they need from each other. Listen to both staff members before commenting on the situation. They will each have their own 'truth'. Use the exercises and skills given to you later in this chapter under 'conflict' with one individual. This will help you to speak directly to both the people involved. They will also know where you stand on the issue. By managing such a meeting, conflict should disappear and staff can then get on with what they are paid to do.

Conflict within a team

There can be conflict within a team. There is little to be gained from listening to everyone complaining about an individual if you do nothing about it. So yes, you do say something and don't ignore it. Inform individuals that you intend to resolve the conflict and that you expect them to speak out.

Bring the team together and praise work that has been carried out successfully, then offer the group the chance to discuss any conflicts they have with each other. Staff must address each other and not speak through you. They talk to the person – not about them. For example, they must not say 'Well, what I think Susan needs is ...'. Instead they must look at Susan, saying, 'Susan, I think you need to ...'

If this open process is too daunting for you, then you could try to put the team in pairs and ask them to address each other individually in the following way:

EXERCISE 4

● ●

Two people sit opposite each other. Let us call them Sarah and Norman. Sarah speaks first and Norman listens, but Norman is not allowed to speak or justify his behaviour, or question what is being said to him. Then the process is reversed. Norman speaks to Sarah and again Sarah may not respond. After the exercise, both Norman and Sarah can discuss what has been revealed to each of them. The format of the exercise is to complete the following sentences, briefly, concisely and above all, honestly, saying:

'I work well with you when _____

_____

_____

_____

_____

'I would work better with you if _____

_____

_____

_____

_____

Do not allow deviation from this wording. Each member of the team is likely to gain some insight into their behaviour. This skill sounds very simple, but it can also be very powerful. For example, Sarah might say:

'I work well with you when . . . you bring work back to me that I have given you and suggest new ideas which you think might be better.'

'I would work better with you if . . . instead of grumbling to other people about me, you came and told me to my face when I have done something to annoy you.'

No comment made by Susan – just accepting what has been said.

Then it is her turn to receive feedback and insight.

Norman might say:

'I work well with you when . . . you discuss your thoughts with me about the new plans for expansion.'

'I would work better with you if . . . you praised me and the other staff more often when they have done a good job. That would make us all feel more valued and motivated.'

If both these suggestions make you nervous, maybe you could initiate some staff training on Team Building.

Conflict within the organization

You may encounter conflict between yourself and *the organization*. You could find yourself out of step with the work ethos and your own value system. A new strategic plan, or a management reorganization, or financial cutbacks, may imply to you that the organization has different priorities from those in which you believe.

This may mean that you have to do something about it. Either you decide to look for another post or rethink your role, relationships, responsibilities or career prospects. It is soul-destroying to try to manage people in an atmosphere where you feel conflict with the organization. The only chance you have is to manage your own inner conflict, conflict between others, and speak up at any meetings in which you feel that the organization is being unjust. Remember an organization is made up of individuals, so you as an individual should take some responsibility for the way in which the organization is behaving.

Conflict with one other person

Conflict can arise between yourself and only one other person. How do you sort out this type of conflict? Does your behaviour differ according to the person's status, role, gender, race, disability, age, or the intimacy of relationship? You are likely to manage people in different ways according to their ability, role or area of responsibility. However, when it comes to managing conflict between yourself and anyone else, regardless of status or relationship, the same format is useful.

The most important point is that you should feel equal to the person concerned. Do not invest power in the other person or you will become submissive. By the same token, do not consider yourself to be all-powerful or you will become aggressive. You have to manage the conflict from an ego state of 'I'm OK', 'You're OK'.

Let us take a simple example of lateness. You decide to do something about it and say, 'Different staff members have told me that you are always late, and it had better stop!' You have lost because the conflict worsens as you are asked, 'Who told you that?' The staff member suspects everyone, which demotivates them. The justification comes with, 'Anyway, they are lying, I'm not always late, I have been on time every day this week. In fact, I was the first person here on Tuesday and Wednesday'. They are right, because if you use the word 'always' you are likely to be wrong.

Developing your language skills for managing conflict
So what are the necessary skills? They are very simple, remember three words, OBSERVE, FEEL, NEED, and use the following guidelines for managing the conflict.

EXERCISE 5
● ●

First, think of a conflict situation. It is important to use a current situation and not one that has been resolved a long time ago, or that was never resolved and has been forgotten. Now complete the following sentences making them relevant to the conflict situation you have in mind.

What I have OBSERVED _____

_____

_____

That makes me FEEL _____

_____

_____

What I NEED is _____

_____

_____

Example: manager and colleague.

Manager: 'What I have observed ... is that you came to work one hour late on Wednesday and Thursday morning of last week – and you returned from your lunchbreak half an hour late on Tuesday and Wednesday without giving me any reasons. That makes me feel upset and what I need is for you to be here on time each morning to support the other staff. If you are going to be late, please inform me, preferably beforehand, or else when you arrive.' Now, think of your own example of an unresolved conflict that you have to manage. Jot it down in the following format, think about it and then practise saying out loud what you want to say.

What I have OBSERVED _____

_____

_____

_____

That makes me FEEL _____

_____

_____

What I NEED is _____

_____

_____

By saying what I have OBSERVED, you avoid being questioned on 'who told you?', so the person feels less threatened.

By disclosing your feelings, no one can argue with how you FEEL but they can argue with how you THINK. They cannot say 'You don't feel angry or concerned', or whatever feeling you are experiencing. Be honest about your feelings. It takes a good secure manager to disclose their feelings. Expressing feelings is not a sign of weakness, but a sign of strength. Beware of avoiding feeling by stating, 'That makes me feel we have a problem' or 'I feel that you have to try harder'. Those are not feelings but rather 'thoughts' and a misuse of the word 'feel'.

By stating what you NEED you let the person know where they stand, what they have to do, how they have to behave, and what is acceptable and what is inappropriate. Too often, managers go all around the houses trying to get to the point but omit to state their actual needs.

How to manage criticism

There will be times when you are criticized, so it is important that you are able to handle criticism in a way that is productive to both you and the critic.

Having explored how to give and receive feedback, you are now probably able to recognize that critical feedback can help you to grow and become more aware of how your behaviour affects others. However, if you are simply criticized, then you will need to know how to access and internalize that information.

First of all you will need to decide if the criticism is valid or invalid. For example:

'You never meet deadlines ...'

Valid?   Yes? Then agree.

Invalid?   Yes? So say so and say why it is invalid or ask the person to be more specific. 'Tell me what deadlines I have failed to meet ...'

Instead of what can often happen:

Critic: 'You never meet deadlines!'

You: 'Oh yes I do, it's just that you expect more and more of me and if I had more resources I could get the job done quicker. It's impossible trying to work to deadlines here because so many staff are either off sick or are sent to work off-site and nobody knows where they are or when they are returning. I can never get in touch with them to get the information I require to finish my report ...' and so on ...

You have resorted to defending and justifying your behaviour. Remember that you have the following options:

As well as receiving criticism you may have to criticize others. Be specific, give instances rather than being vague. Comment on *behaviour* that can be changed, rather than on the person themselves. Recognize that you may be wrong and that the other person could have a good and valid reason for what has happened; you will not know about it unless you ask.

Here is a useful diagram to show the various options:

Diagram 4

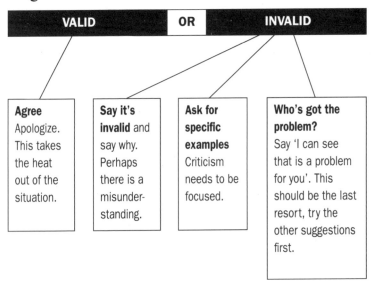

VALID	OR	INVALID

| **Agree** Apologize. This takes the heat out of the situation. | **Say it's invalid** and say why. Perhaps there is a misunderstanding. | **Ask for specific examples** Criticism needs to be focused. | **Who's got the problem?** Say 'I can see that is a problem for you'. This should be the last resort, try the other suggestions first. |

Managing conflict when you are criticized

How do you react to criticism? Some people start to justify their behaviour while others say nothing but feel angry or upset. Others respond by blaming someone else.

EXERCISE 6

● ●

Think of an example when someone has criticized you:

1   What exactly did they say?

_____

_____

2   How did you respond?

_____

_____

3   What was the outcome?

_____

_____

Now ask yourself . . .

4   Was the criticism valid or invalid?

_____

_____

5   If it was valid, did you agree with them?

_____

_____

6   If it was invalid did you disagree with the person and say why it was invalid?

_____

_____

7   Was the criticism vague?

_____

_____

8   Did you ask them to give you specific examples of their criticism of your behaviour?

_____

_____

9   Who had the problem?

_____

_____

10   What could you do differently next time?

_____

_____

SUMMARY

Having recognized your management style for conflict, maybe you can now work at addressing difficult issues, working towards a WIN-WIN situation. That is, rather than attacking, adapting or trying to accommodate or avoid.

When you are experiencing inner conflict (what you want as against what is expected of you) see if the options exercise can help. You may not like to take the time in completing it, but you could save yourself a lot more time and energy by doing so.

In effectively managing your team, you need the skills to speak to them both as individuals and as a group. You are doing yourself no favours by talking about people rather than to them.

In order to manage organizational conflict, you will just need to keep chipping away at the aspects that affect you. Be an assertive voice – heard at meetings, in the social areas and, more importantly, with the individuals that make up the organization.

By managing conflict with any single person, be it one of your staff or your senior managers, you will find that resolving it brings an inner calmness.

You will feel much more positive about yourself and are likely to be amazed at how the other person has been feeling. So remember the three trigger words: Observe, Feel and Need.

Nobody is perfect; every manager makes mistakes. So when you are criticized, recall the simple tip of asking yourself, 'Is this a valid or invalid criticism?' and you now know how to respond. If you have forgotten, refer back and use that other skill you have acquired of 'checking it out'.

CHAPTER 5

Is it because they can't — or is it because they won't?

Now that you understand why you relate better to some members of staff
than to others, and are able to manage
conflict more effectively, you can
move on to managing 'marginal performers', that is, people
who are performing below an expected standard.

'Marginal performer' can sound a derogatory term but it is
not meant to be. It is a kind of shorthand for someone whose
performance is of a borderline nature. It implies someone
who is performing below or just on a given benchmark. This
could be a temporary situation, and I believe all managers at
some point in their lives perform in a marginal way. They just
about keep the job ticking over, not really innovating or
stretching their energy levels, but simply turning up to work,
going through the processes and going home. Maybe some of
you think that the latter is all that you are supposed to do.
Some staff's performance may vary widely from day to day,
others may be experiencing personal difficulties that you

know about, which means that for a period of time they are not performing up to standard. Have you inherited a marginal performer? If so, for how long have you been managing them? If for more than three months, then you should already have done something about it. You must address the problem yourself and take responsibility for finding a solution. Let us begin by looking at your staff and considering a natural distribution curve of their performance.

Diagram 5: Distribution curve of your staff's performance

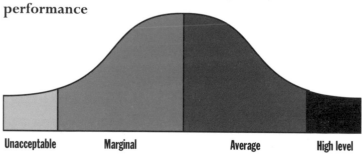

Unacceptable   **Marginal**   **Average**   **High level**

This figure shows that 2–3 per cent of your staff work really well while 2–3 per cent of your staff work in a less than acceptable way. This figure also shows that half your staff work below average. As least it does mathematically, but this is not normally the case. It is more likely to look something like diagram 6.

Diagram 6: Likely curve of staff performance

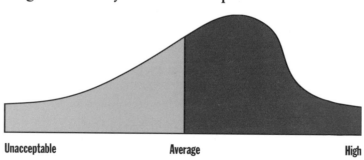

Unacceptable   **Average**   **High**

People move around the performance levels according to job motivation and personal issues and concerns. Losing a job interview, status, power or a team mate can temporarily demotivate someone, but they may quickly return to a higher level of performance. You need to know your reasons for judging someone as a marginal performer. What yardstick are you using – your own performance or that of the rest of the team? (See diagram 7.)

Diagram 7

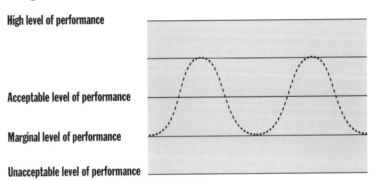

High level of performance

Acceptable level of performance

Marginal level of performance

Unacceptable level of performance

Having identified what is meant by a 'marginal performer' or someone who is performing in a marginal way, decide if it is because they can't or won't do better. If they can't, it is a matter of competence, whereas if they won't, a course of disciplinary action is called for. Staff can be assisted to improve their performance by effective staff training, but it is also up to you to establish the causes and effects on yourself and others and to be able to act accordingly.

This chapter focuses on the indicators of marginal performers and analyzes possible reasons for such behaviour. This includes your management approach and organizational causes and provides processes and procedures for dealing with these issues. It shows how you need to address the possibility of any organizational process that may have contributed to the situation. A checklist is included for your consideration.

So let us begin by raising your awareness and trying to identify the signs of marginal performers and organizational causes of marginal performance. First complete Questionnaire 7 and then read the analysis and consider the checklist for possible organizational causes that may contribute to your staff performing in a marginal manner.

QUESTIONNAIRE 7
Identifying the reasons

● ●

Think of a member of staff who you believe is not performing up to your standards in his or her job. Try to identify exactly what are the indicators of their marginal performance. Tick the following appropriate boxes:

		Yes	No
1	Has their appearance changed?	☐	☐
2	Are they behaving differently?	☐	☐
3	Have they been dishonest?	☐	☐
4	Are they slow in making decisions?	☐	☐
5	Is there conflict between them and other members of staff?	☐	☐
6	Are they frequently absent from work?	☐	☐
7	Is their quantity of work deteriorating?	☐	☐
8	Is their quality of work deteriorating?	☐	☐
9	Are they experiencing personal problems or concerns?	☐	☐
10	Does their behaviour detrimentally affect others?	☐	☐

If any member of staff gains three or more 'yes' answers, then you have a marginal performer to manage. But remember that just one 'yes' answer could signal problems that may soon arise, and action now may prevent matters from getting worse.

■ ANALYSIS OF QUESTIONNAIRE 7

Indicators of marginal performers

Having focused on specific issues, now think about how you have been managing that person.

People's appearance or behaviour can change for the worse when they are depressed, losing their self-love or self-respect, though this is not the only indication of 'poor self-worth'. Conversely, some people need to be meticulous on the outside, which conceals internal problems. Disturbed children can be very neat in how they fold their clothes and organize their possessions: it is as if having the outside of their lives organized helps them with their inside confusion. You may have heard of the obsessive housewife/house-husband who appears neurotic to others because the house has to be immaculate. Don't be fooled! Despite the pristine outward appearance, this could be an indication that chaos reigns within.

If you observe someone's appearance or behaviour change, be aware that this may be temporary. There may be many reasons for the alteration you perceive, such as a new relationship, financial changes or even moving house. They may feel resentful because of missed promotion, or maybe they have been superseded by someone whom they consider to be their junior or inferior. Personal problems could also be to blame. Be sure you are seeing the situation accurately.

If you suspect that someone is being dishonest, it is essential to collect evidence, since this behaviour is highly likely to lead to dismissal.

If your cause for concern is slowness in making decisions, it could be that the person concerned is unsure of their power. You may have delegated work to them, but not empowered them to make decisions. They may be unsure of your response to any indication of decision-making on their part. Do you tend to criticize, or are they confident that you will back their decisions?

If there is conflict between them and others, you will need to address that conflict as demonstrated in the previous chapter.

If staff are frequently absent, keep an accurate record of their absence. Again, this may lead to a first warning of dismissal, so evidence is important as you may have to defend yourself or your company at an Industrial Tribunal.

When you believe that quantity or quality of work is deteriorating, ask yourself if you are seeking unachievable standards. Have you been giving your staff regular feedback? Communication is a wonderful thing. Try asking for feedback, because changes in your attitude or behaviour may be contributing to the problem that your team is facing.

Staff experiencing personal concerns need your help and attention. Check out if there are possible reasons for unacceptable behaviour by using and practising the skills in listening and managing conflict that you have acquired.

The behaviour of each member of your staff team is likely to affect colleagues, both advantageously and detrimentally. The latter needs addressing: your management skills are being tested. Often present behaviour may reflect the fact that you have been managing ineffectively and have been ignoring unacceptable behaviour for some time. Your staff may now consider that the very behaviour you are objecting to has, in fact, become custom and practice.

Having looked at how you, as an individual, manage your team, it may be worthwhile considering whether any problem situation is exacerbated by the company's organizational structure, procedures and/or processes. Consider the following possibilities:

Possible organizational causes that can produce marginal performance

Your organization may be responsible for some of the reasons why your staff are becoming marginal performers. This could mean YOU.

Check list

1   Bad selection procedures. If the organization has appointed unsuitable staff, then management should find a way of rectifying their mistakes.

2   Poor interviewing techniques and procedures.

3   A lack of induction. How people start their job affects their expectations of the job.

4   Inadequate supervision, coaching, counselling, controlling or directing.

5   Poor appraisal skills or a lack of a policy for appraisal.

6   Poor working conditions – psychological or behavioural. Worrying about people's behaviour at work can create stress for them which can lower performance. Bullying or chauvinistic behaviour can be a problem. Poor physical working conditions, such as dim lighting and inadequate air conditioning or dirty surroundings, can lead to a downgrading of performance.

7   A tolerance of poor standards. People come to consider it customary practice.

8   Too much organizational change for change's sake.

9   Organizational changes which mean that they have new working practices.

10 Management reorganization, loss of status, power or a prime seating place in the office.

11 Change through external pressure – the need for performance indicators to be met.

12 Change in the nature of the clients being served.

13 In the reflection of society. There is a smaller proportion of the population actually in work. Most people are working harder than those of a generation ago. Those working below this new level are now regarded as marginal performers.

14 Rumours of redundancies leading to a feeling of insecurity of position.

15 Lack of tenure – today virtually no one can be guaranteed a job for life.

16 Personal circumstances outside work.

17 Individuals change with the passage of time (values change).

18 Ineffective management and leadership by their line manager, but nothing is done about it.

19 Being on the receiving end of poor management as a result of a poor line manager.

20 Infrequent, unprofessional or a complete lack of training. Almost all staff improve with effective training.

◼ Deciding if they can't or won't

A member of your staff is not achieving and/or maintaining a standard of performance that is acceptable to you. So first you have to decide if it is because they 'can't' or because they 'won't'. (See diagram 8)

Diagram 8

Disciplinary action?

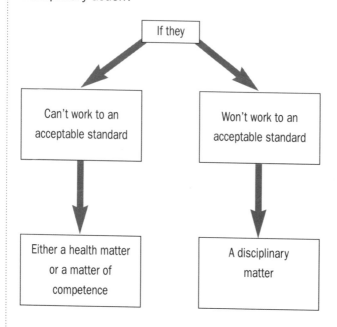

■ Issues of competence or capability

If it is a health matter, you will need to give support and gather medical evidence. Some health matters are temporary but with others it may mean that the staff member has to leave on the grounds of ill health.

If it is a matter of competence or capability then you may need to consider the options you have. These could include using your supportive and helping skills; setting targets and monitoring them, reducing stress, redesigning their job, having regular counselling, or proposing a leaving or retirement package.

It will not help, however, to *promote* someone who is underachieving to another position. This can create a lot of unease among other staff. Just as promoting someone is unhelpful in these circumstances, so is *demoting* someone. The idea behind this is that if they cannot manage one job they might be able to manage another. This is highly unlikely unless they are given support and the change is supported by colleagues and the rest of the team.

Also you will not help by *ignoring* the situation in the hope that it will go away. It is hardly likely to and is much more likely to be exacerbated. You may also be giving other staff members the message that it is acceptable to behave in such a way and soon other colleagues could be operating in the same manner. Hence the phrase 'Well it is customary to do that here'. You would be very likely to lose at any tribunal where such a statement was used in defence.

What to do when they can't?

When you have decided that someone cannot do their job you will need *evidence* of their lack of capability; for example, poor work output or administration. You will need to investigate the situation and surrounding circumstances. You can do nothing without recent evidence and must gain it before taking action. You will need to inform the employee personally about their shortcomings. You could offer training, counselling or supervision but should also warn them of the consequences if no improvement is made.

You will need to give them *formal assistance* and monitor their progress and keep a *written record of the assistance* that you have given with a progress report.

If the employee then improves their performance there could be no need for any further action. If they do not improve, you may need to convene a formal disciplinary interview and, if appropriate, apply the warning procedure as in the Disciplinary Procedure. This formally warns the employee of failure to improve. If no improvement occurs, it is correct to recommend dismissal You must take all action in line with company policy and check each stage with the personnel department.

What do I do when they won't?

If the member of staff will not do what is requested of them, you have only one option – which is to go down the disciplinary road. The disciplinary interview should make it easier for you to tell the person exactly what is expected of them although often the disciplinary process is used as a precursor to getting rid of problem personnel.

An effective manager needs to learn from this experience in order to prevent similar contentious issues reoccurring. Few managers are able to go through such a process unscarred.

Let us take this procedure step by step. To begin with, you need to identify the problem and assemble the facts. Then you must decide upon the appropriate action to take. You have a choice of four actions. One, do nothing; two, give training; three, offer counselling; or four, discipline.

1 If you decide to *do nothing* then at least keep a record of the situation and your decision to end the action.

2 If you assess that some form of *training* is the best decision, identify the right type and content of the training needed. Then jointly arrange a suitable programme, course or conference and monitor the person's progress. Set up an interview to discuss how the training is going and what learning has taken place and

how that learning can affect their job. Keep a record of your monitoring and assessment. If there is an improvement, the action ends but if not you will need to continue with the disciplinary procedure.

3 If you think offering *counselling* will be the best path of action, you will need to find a suitable person to whom to refer the employee. Some companies have people within the firm while others use outside agencies. Again you will need to monitor progress, and there the action ends.

4 If *discipline* is your decision, you will have to set up an interview and make a final decision as to whether more training or disciplinary action might work as a last resort. If you decided that you are going down the disciplinary route, then you need to be certain about the procedure.

This is how you deal with the disciplinary procedure. Initially you can do one of three things depending on the behaviour or offence.

1 Give an *oral warning*.

2 Give a *written warning*.

3 *Dismiss immediately* on the gounds of gross misconduct, demote or suspend without pay.

After the *oral warning* monitor the situation. If there is improvement no further action may be needed. But if no improvement has taken place then you offer the *first written warning*. Depending on the reaction, you may decide to take no more action or to issue the *second written warning*.

Again monitor and then decide whether to take further action or to issue the *final written warning*. Having monitored that situation again, decide whether to end the action or dismiss the employee.

Diagram 9: Dismissal procedure

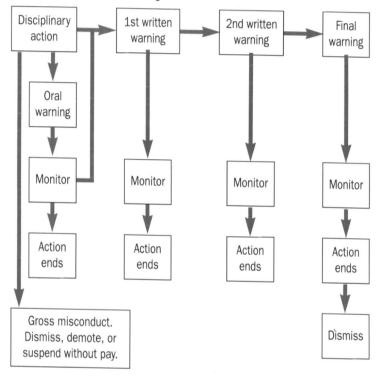

Always remember to work closely with the personnel department and seek legal advice before you embark on a disciplinary route. Tribunals are stressful and should be avoided where possible in the interests of employer and employee.

EXERCISE 7
Categorizing disciplinary offences
● ●

Disciplinary offences

Let us now summarize and see if you remember the different stages and what you might do in certain work situations.

When a member of your staff is involved in behaviour which is not deemed acceptable there are four likely outcomes:

Non-acceptable behaviour (NAB)

As its title suggests, this is behaviour which is not acceptable but which is not considered to be serious and will not warrant an official warning. Nevertheless, in any organization you have a duty as a manager to address anyone whose behaviour is not acceptable.

Official warning (OW)

Official warnings are part of the disciplinary procedure. The misdemeanour is considered serious enough to be recorded after you have given your member of staff an official oral warning.

Formal written warning (WW)

First-stage interview: applicable where the conduct complained of is more serious than an Official Warning, or where an Official Warning has been ignored. A first-stage disciplinary interview needs to be held.

Further or gross misconduct (GM)

Second-stage interview: this should be used where there is reason to believe that gross misconduct has taken place, or after an official written warning has been ignored. A second-stage disciplinary interview needs to be held. A likely outcome could be permanent exclusion from work.

Categorising disciplinary offences

Below is a list of ten misdemeanours. In each example you have access only to the information given and you would generally ensure that you have further information before reaching a decision; nevertheless you will have a view as to the seriousness of the misdemeanour.

The exercise is to categorize the ten misdemeanours using the following four categories:

Non-acceptable behaviour	**NAB**
Official warning	**OW**
Formal written warning	**WW**
Further or gross misconduct	**GM**

When you have completed the task you may like to compare your decision with that of other working colleagues. Different managers have different values and work in different ways, but certainly some of the examples below involve gross misconduct and to deal with the situation you would need to become familiar with the disciplinary procedure. Write in the box the intials that you think most apply (NAB, OW, WW or GM).

1   In spite of continuous reminders, a member
    of staff persists in handing in work for a
    project a week late. This has been happening
    for two months.

2   A member of staff has reported in sick but
    is seen on the same day in a golf tournament.

3   A member of staff is suspected by one of
    the IT team of introducing a computer
    virus into the network.

4   A member of staff is observed smoking
    in a designated non-smoking area during a
    ten-minute break.

5   A member of the cleaning staff told you that
    one of your staff was seen dropping unsightly
    litter and when asked to pick it up, the
    alleged person refused to pick it up, saying
    it was the cleaner's job.

6   You have overheard a member of staff
    making comments about another staff
    member's sexual orientation deliberately
    to cause offence.

7   You walk into a work area to find one
    member of staff violently punching another
    person, who is desperately trying to
    defend himself. Later you find a knife
    in the offender's pocket.

8   Money has gone missing from the staff
    cloakroom on three occasions. Now a
    member of staff is brought to you having
    being seen going through people's
    coat pockets.

9   The local weekly newspaper contains an
    article on serious vandalism on a local estate.
    The report states that police proceedings
    are taking place against two young persons
    and you realize that one of the suspects
    works in your organization.

10 You are told that one of the female staff
    claims to have been sexually abused by
    a male member of the management team.

Hopefully, you will now be able to recognize the different
level of disciplinary procedures that would be necessary in
each of these situations. It is always worth seeking advice and
help from colleagues. As an effective manager, you will know
that disciplinary hearings and tribunals are a last resort and
that the correct action taken at the right time can defuse
many problem situations.

Burn out or rust out?

It is quite possible, of course, that the member of staff in
question has quite simply reached the stage of 'burn out' or
'rust out', in which event you will have some serious thinking
to do. 'Burn out' is when someone is performing below an
acceptable level through stress and pressure of work. 'Rust

out' is when someone is stressed through boredom and too *little* work: being underworked and undervalued can be more stressful than being overworked.

You will need to consider and assess, for example, the length of service the employee has given to the company; what their age is; what the current labour market situation is for your member of staff, and so on.

You will also have to consider the effect their present behaviour is having on other members of staff and what the reaction of work colleagues would be if, say, the person in question was dismissed or given early retirement.

Possibly your staff would be greatly relieved if someone left the team in this way and might subsequently pull together far more efficiently. But, human nature being what it is, the marginal performer may get a 'sympathy vote' from colleagues that would involve you in yet more disruption and unrest.

If a member of your team is suffering from burn out, then they may welcome your intervention and be hoping for some kind of financial package that will allow them to leave or move to a less stressful job in the company. You owe it to your staff to consider their general health and welfare as well as their actual performance.

CONCLUSION

So what is meant by managing people effectively? And how may this book have affected your management of people?

By now you will know that you need to look as though you enjoy interacting with other people. In this way you will actually enhance the relationship, moving on to a better understanding of your staff's needs and in so doing will be more likely to enhance their work output. In order to be able to do this you have learned how to build on the strengths of your staff and give them support when it is needed.

Having looked at some of the reasons for relating positively and negatively towards some of your staff, you are likely now to be aware of the importance of value systems and how they can affect the way in which you relate better to some staff and less well to others. Possibly you could be checking out your value systems with all kinds of people, maybe sometimes asking yourself 'On what values are they basing such a comment?'

Ideally, you will now be able to manage all your staff in as fair a way as possible. You will be aware that your own values and belief systems may affect how you manage your staff. As you discover what your own feelings of anxiety are, you will learn how to use the exercise to identify 'shadows', which may now make life easier for you. Also you will probably recognize that some of the staff you had difficulties in relating to may have had shadows you can now recognize.

Perhaps by now you are aware of how you stereotype people according to their physical appearance, the language they use, their religion, race, roles, sexual orientation, gender or the attitudes they hold. However, awareness is not enough. You need to do something about it. Maybe you no longer attribute certain concepts to someone's physical appearance or the way in which they dress. Hopefully you are finding that you are more tolerant in your attitudes to other people.

By now you will guard against remarks made through ignorance, or in malice, that may offend some of your staff, and be aware of the importance of the language you use. For instance, not talking about 'coloured' people, but using the word 'black', or referring to their nationality, like Caribbean, Indian and African. Using the term 'first name' rather than 'Christian name' since many people are not Christians.

This does not mean that you have to be vigorously politically correct, but you must recognize that certain words do offend. Talking in terms of people working 'with' you, rather than 'for' you creates a whole different set of feelings. Some words are powerful and some are derogatory like 'subordinate' or 'minion', which can deflate your staff and shows your formal arrogance as their manager.

When you are able to treat people as equals you will be more effective. Your staff may have unequal salaries, unequal jobs, unequal status, unequal power, but they are all equal in how they feel. Virtually all people feel hurt if criticized, threatened by fear if redundancy looms, or encouraged and valued when praised.

Having recognized your conflict-management style, you could now be addressing, arbitrating and resolving conflict when it occurs, rather than avoiding it or worrying what people might think of you.

Constantly adapting or compromising in conflict situations does not bring about harmony. Nor does attacking people. So remember that both parties need to feel positive.

When other people have conflicts with you and criticize, you know how to establish whether it is valid or invalid and respond appropriately.

The frustrations that you have felt about certain members of staff may now be easier, as you can ascertain what might be the cause of their not performing up to standard: whether it is because of the organizational practices or your management style. You are probably able by now to establish whether it is because they can't or won't, and act accordingly.

Above all, the fact that you have bothered to find out about how to manage people effectively, shows that you care and want to improve your management skills.

Notes

Notes